Admit it!

Admit it!

✦

21 things you already know but apparently have forgotten regarding client service

Craig S. Galati

iUniverse, Inc.
New York Lincoln Shanghai

Admit it!
21 things you already know but apparently have forgotten regarding client service

iUniverse books may be ordered through booksellers or by contacting:

iUniverse
2021 Pine Lake Road, Suite 100
Lincoln, NE 68512
www.iuniverse.com
1-800-Authors (1-800-288-4677)

ISBN-13: 978-0-595-37365-9 (pbk)
ISBN-13: 978-0-595-81762-7 (ebk)
ISBN-10: 0-595-37365-8 (pbk)
ISBN-10: 0-595-81762-9 (ebk)

Printed in the United States of America

Contents

But First…

A strange thing happened on the way through the 90's. Professional service firms quit delivering the quality customer service that clients of previous generations had received. I remember recently a client thanked me for calling him back. I was surprised, so I asked what compelled him to thank me for doing what I considered a common courtesy. "You'd be surprised," he said, "at how many days go by before some of my most trusted consultants call me back, even if I say it's important."

This conversation made me look around at my office, my staff, and the people with whom I did business. What I noticed is that people generally provided mediocre service, at best. I talked to some of my staff about it, and it seemed that they hadn't had many good role models. They had not been mentored by someone who had a passion for delivering solid, no-nonsense, excellent customer service—the kind that makes you thank someone for caring.

I decided to become that mentor, and that is why I wrote this book. I began devouring books such as "Discovering the Soul of Service," "The Invisible Touch," and "Life's Little Instruction Book." I studied Robert Greenleaf's famous essay on servant leadership. I realized that if I expected my staff to provide exceptional customer service, we needed to define it and we needed to develop some fundamental guidelines to help us achieve that goal.

Those guidelines became the outline for a small desktop reference pamphlet, a PowerPoint staff meeting presentation, and the basis for this book.

I'm not sure what caused this slip in professional service, but I'm determined not to let it happen in my office. I hope this book will be a useful tool for your office as well. I offer this book to share these simple, yet essential ideas—ideas that will lead to better client service, better client retention, and a more rewarding experience for you, your clients, and your staff. Our experience has proved it will lead to repeat business and help in developing lifelong client relationships.

Throughout this book, I will share with you the good, the bad, and the ugly. Some of these experiences are directly from my work; others I have adapted from stories that I was told by friends and colleagues, and some I have observed in my daily travels.

Craig

Acknowledgments

I would like to thank my wife, Sally, and my two sons, Corin and Carson, who have always been on my side. Thanks, guys!

Special thanks to Cindy, who truly understands customer service.

Thanks to Annita and Valerie, who encouraged me throughout the writing of this book.

Finally, special thanks to Veronica, Julie, and Harry, who helped me wrap this book up with a nice bow.

Thanks all!

Craig

1

Treat clients the way they want to be treated

How many times have you been treated by one of your consultants as if he was doing you a favor? Is that the way you want to be treated? Of course not.

I particularly recall a technology consultant who treated us as if we should be thankful he was taking time from his busy schedule to consult with us. While his technical expertise was valuable, he didn't treat us the way we wanted to be treated. We wanted to know that he cared about our business at least as much as he cared about his own.

Just as patients expect their doctor to have empathy for them when they are ill, clients want to be treated like their business matters. There is no doubt you are busy and your time is valuable, but your clients need to know that you are involved with their projects because you want to be, not because you have to be. Show some enthusiasm; servicing clients is fun!

On one occasion, a young staff member complained that he wasn't connecting with a client the way he wanted to. I asked him if he had ever talked to the client about this. He said there was never time. "The client meetings are only once a week and by the time we get through the issues at hand, I need to run to my next meeting," he said.

Through dialogue, we began to break down the issues. The client was an older gentleman, with a very laid-back style. The young architect was a 25-year-old kid, full of vigor and energy, the kind of energy most people want on their project. I suggested that maybe this energy was being misconstrued and that maybe the client felt rushed and unimportant. The young architect went back to the client, this time with a different approach. They talked about the issue and the client stated that he had always given his full attention to his own clients and never was in a hurry to get to the next meeting. He gave his clients all the time they needed and this was how he wanted to be treated.

An important lesson was learned that day: you can't assume to know how the client wants to be treated unless you ask.

Treat clients the way THEY want to be treated.

2

Make repeat business and referrals your goal

Have you ever referred a person to someone else? When you do, you now have a vested interest in the success of the referral. People don't give referrals lightly. When a client refers you or engages you for a second time, that is the ultimate compliment.

Good client service that leads to a second opportunity or to a referral increases the profitability of your firm. There are no marketing costs, no cold calls, just the opportunity to continue or build a new relationship. According to the Society for Marketing Professional Services, a majority of firms spend between four and five percent of their gross revenue attracting new customers. In my experience, it costs anywhere from six to ten times more to acquire a new client than to retain a current one.

Keeping existing clients and contracting with them for repeat business therefore makes a significant difference to your profitability.

In addition, when you get the chance to do a second project for an existing client, there is the opportunity to deliver even better service than you did the first time. You know the client and you know his expectations; now is the time to exceed those expectations.

3

If the client looks good, you look good

Make your client look good all of the time and you will have that client for life.

Most people want to do a good job; and just like you, your client also wants his project to come out well. That is why you have been trusted to help him achieve his goals.

I recall a recent client who fought hard for us get a project with his company. It didn't take me long to realize that he wanted us because he had developed trust in us—and that this project was very important for his success and eventual promotion within his company.

He had a stake in our performance and he gave our firm a tremendous opportunity. All we had to do was make sure his project went well and we both would benefit.

The project was completed well and our client did receive the promotion. He is now in a position to directly make the decisions with the firms his company does business with, and he didn't forget how we helped him look good.

4

Get to know who the "real" client is

Have you ever thought you provided exemplary service to a client only to find out that the needs you met weren't the needs of the organization, but were instead the needs of the client representative? An experience like this will teach you a lot.

I remember designing a treatment plant for a major local water purveyor. One of the goals of the project was to create a special experience at the plant to educate the public on water issues.

Through our discovery process working with senior managers, it was determined that water conservation was the most important message to be conveyed. We designed a pavilion around the theme of conservation as part of a public tour route—the culmination of the public experience. We designed areas where ways to conserve were described. We included examples of water conserving plant materials and graphs which showed how much water would be conserved if everyone in the valley did certain things. We were really proud of our work. Along with the management team, we had a winner on our hands. We couldn't wait to present it to the Director and the County Commission.

However, as we presented the concepts and walked them through our ideas, a silence hung over the room—the kind of silence where you know you have either showed up at the wrong meeting or are very much off the mark. The Director broke the silence. "Water conservation is important, but the whole purpose of this plant is about water quality, that's the message we want the public to go home with, that the water is of the highest standard."

We were sent back to the drawing board.

Take the time needed to completely understand the engagement you are beginning. Who makes the decisions? How are those decisions made? Does the client representative really represent the client?

Get to know who really calls the shots.

5

Make it easy for your clients to describe you as excellent

If you ever had a chance to write your own letter of recommendation, what would you say about yourself? Would you describe yourself as responsive, honest, and trustworthy? Every time you work with a client, you have the opportunity to influence that letter of recommendation.

Deliver the service that makes it easy for your client to describe you the way you want to be described.

Create your self-fulfilling prophecy every time you conduct business.

6

Never say "no"

I actually heard one of our staff members tell a client "no," without even taking the time to think about what was being requested. I was appalled. This incident provided an excellent opportunity to teach how our firm conducts business.

While you can't say "yes" to everything all of the time, the first response should never be no. Think it over. Can you do what the client requested? Is there another way to accomplish the client's objectives? Do you have a good understanding of what the client really wants and needs?

I've found that clients ask for a lot of things not fully understanding what the request entails. I do, too. It's our job as consultants to figure out how to best meet client needs and to provide them with alternatives to meet those needs.

Nothing stops the dialogue or strains a relationship like the word "no."

7

Go out of your way, all the time

Going out of your way to provide exceptional customer service is not as difficult as it sounds. Once you decide you want to provide excellence, it will become natural.

We had a client for whom we were doing a small project. While our Project Architect was at the client's office discussing the project, he learned that our client had retained another consultant to design the remodel of his home. The client was preparing to submit the drawings of his house remodel to the local building department on his own (I'm not sure why his other consultant wasn't handling this task). We were ready to submit our drawings at the same time.

Our Project Architect didn't hesitate to offer to submit both projects for the client. To the client this seemed like a simple task; the Project Architect was going there already. But the projects were in two different jurisdictions which required two stops and two different submittal procedures. This didn't dampen our Project Architect's spirits—he submitted both and the client was delighted.

That is what I call going out of your way. I'm sure our client will remember that gesture, but that is not why our Project Architect did it. He did it because he was there to service the client and make his life easier. I'm convinced that this small task reflected well on both the Project Architect and our firm, and I'm very proud of that.

Going out of your way doesn't always mean doing difficult things; most of the time it's doing the simple things like dropping something off, bringing the client that extra copy of the material so he doesn't need to copy it for internal circulation, offering to help him prepare for a tough meeting, or sending him that article you know he will love.

8

Never forget that all of your actions contribute to the customer experience

The customer experience is shaped by many factors, including, for example, the way you answer the phone, the way clients are greeted, and how promptly you return a phone call.

All too often, many professionals forget that ALL of their actions contribute to the customer experience. You don't get to choose which actions have a positive impression on your client. Think of how you feel when you are interacting with your attorney or your accountant. Do they send you mixed signals or do they consistently deliver a strong, customer-focused message in all of their actions?

At one time, I was working with a financial planner who delivered great customer service on a face-to-face basis.

However, he seemed to disappear once he left the meeting. There were times when it took two weeks to get a return call. When he did get around to returning a call, he was great at making me feel good about being his client, but I knew that if I didn't get resolution during the conversation, I would be waiting a long time for the next call.

When I approached him regarding this issue, he told me that he gave me his undivided attention while he was with me, but after he left, he had other clients that required his attention.

Although I understood I was not his only client, I wanted to be treated as if I were. I wanted to know that I was still important to him, even when we weren't meeting face-to-face.

Needless to say, he is now my former financial planner.

9

Don't return calls during lunchtime

Does anyone not know that people who return calls during lunchtime don't really want to talk, but are returning calls only to avoid being known as the person who doesn't return calls? Anyone who's been in business for over five minutes knows this!

When someone needs something from me, they call me when they know I'll be in the office or they call me on my cell phone. But when I need something from them, I often get only a voicemail at the office during the lunch hour, even after I've given them my cell number. I call this phenomenon "call dodging."

Phone tag is going to happen even when both parties are trying to get in touch with each other. Don't make it worse by intentionally calling back when you know someone isn't going to be there.

Clients see right through call dodging.

Don't insult their intelligence.

10

Make your clients feel at home

Ever go to a doctor's office and be forced to wait in a poorly lit, poorly furnished waiting room, then forced into a sterile exam room with no place to sit or wait comfortably? Contrast that with the comfortable seating area of your local Starbucks. Where would you want to return?

The front door and the greeting that clients receive when they come to your office helps set the tone for the relationship you want to develop. Have your receptionist greet them by name, offer them something to drink and make sure they are comfortable.

Never overlook the importance of making a great first impression.

11

Give more than clients expect

Providing what you considered excellent client service and then finding out that you didn't meet the client's expectations is a lesson you need to learn only once. Apparently, you never understood the client's expectations in the first place.

Too often, professionals do not take the time to talk to their clients about their service expectations. But, this is not optional—how can you meet expectations that you don't even know exist, let alone, exceed those expectations?

You must take the time to ask your client about his expectations. How soon does he expect a return phone call? How does he like to communicate? How collaborative is the client? How does he like to make decisions? Where does he place value in your service?

Once you know his expectations, you can meet them, but don't stop there.

Meeting client expectations is not delivering exceptional customer service. It is only by exceeding client expectations that you can provide outstanding customer service.

12

Customer service is not an act or a time of day; it's a lifestyle

I had a friend who bought a new car. He was quite happy with the dealership and was impressed when after a few days, he received a voice message that the dealer was following up on how he was enjoying his new purchase. He couldn't wait to call them back because he knew how much they would appreciate his comments about how well he was treated.

When he returned the call, he was greeted by a much more hurried and flustered woman than the one who had left him the message. "Sir, could you call back tomorrow, I don't do customer service on Wednesdays," was the response he got.

Now, he knew that she meant she did the customer service surveys at scheduled times, but her response did leave an impression, and not a good one.

Remember, customer service is not an act or event; it's not a survey or what's filled out on a form.

Customer service is a way of life; it's a commitment.

13

Return the routine phone calls promptly; return the difficult ones sooner

Most people will readily call a client back when they have good news, but we avoid giving bad news like the plague. We know that bad news, or our perception of bad news, doesn't get better by not delivering it, but we avoid it as long as possible.

Maybe if we thought of returning those tough calls as a way to practice sound client service, we might return them with the same vigor that we call with good news.

Put yourself in the shoes of your client. He's calling you because he needs an answer that only you can provide. Without an answer—any answer—he can't make an informed decision.

There are very few things as important to providing excellent customer service as promptly returning your phone calls and e-mails.

Don't be that person who "never calls back."

14

Keep your promises

Sounds simple, but how often do you keep your promises? Many people make so many promises that they can't keep them all. Why make a promise if you can't keep it? Remember, the most important part of making a promise is fulfilling it and an unfulfilled promise is a betrayal of your client's trust.

I had a recent client tell me that when he called one of our references, he was told, "This firm keeps its promises." That was the reason the client selected us for the project.

People make promises all day, presumably with the intention of keeping them. Those people fail to recognize that breaking a promise is far more damaging to the relationship than never making one at all. When you tell a client that you will complete something by the end of the day Tuesday, that does not mean you have until the start of business on Wednesday to complete the job.

Plan your jobs according to the promises you make and you'll have happy clients.

It takes work and diligence to fulfill your promises. I only promise things that I know I can deliver.

A promise is a commitment. Take a commitment seriously.

15

Thoroughly understand what value means to your clients

Nothing is worse than thinking you did a great job only to discover that you and your client were not on the same page from a "value" perspective. I've noticed that many professionals put a different value on their services than do their clients. This may mean that you and your client are not in alignment, and it is a clear indicator that someone is going to be disappointed in the relationship.

Use your early meetings with a client to understand the items that are important to him and what he perceives as real value. I ask my clients, "What can we do that will make you say, 'Wow that was valuable!'" The client's answer will allow you to understand how you can best work with him. It will also give you clues as to when you will be perceived as bringing him value.

We still remember the young intern in our office that we watched sanding the pieces of a study model he was building. It wasn't that we didn't want him to do a good job, but the purpose of a study model is to quickly convey an idea to "study" if we want to pursue it further. We asked him if he thought sanding the pieces would be of value to our client, and he responded that he really didn't know.

Don't sand the study model unless you know the answer to the question is "yes."

16

Tackle the tough issues face-to-face

As in any relationship, there will be times when you must confront tough issues with your clients. It may involve something you did or did not do, or it might be that you are delivering bad news.

I've found that those issues are best addressed face-to-face rather than over the telephone or through e-mail. Sure, it may be easier for you to deliver bad news without looking into the client's eyes, but you place yourself at a distinct disadvantage when you don't talk directly.

When you meet face-to-face, you can ease into the issue and have the client's undivided attention. You also show your client that you care enough about him to take the time to meet. You will gain credibility and enhance your ability to resolve the problem then and there.

Ever get bad news in a letter? Remember how you felt—how impersonal and unimportant you perceived the message to be?

Don't create that feeling for your clients.

17

Tell the truth always; own up to your own mistakes

Nothing ruins your credibility more than lying to a client. It doesn't just hurt that specific relationship; it also hurts future relationships. Most people would rather know the truth and deal with it than be lied to and still have to deal with the issue later, this time in crisis.

It's so easy in business to get yourself in the situation where a little exaggeration or a white lie will get you out of a jam. The problem is that, in most cases, the client knows when you are not being honest with him.

Early in my career, I worked for a man who was the king of stretching the truth. Over a couple of years, I watched him evolve to the point that he couldn't distinguish between when he was lying and when he was telling the truth. I observed many clients leave the firm, and I heard the ones who stayed laugh out loud when we told them when the work would be completed.

Everyone makes mistakes. A mistake can be fixed once you admit that you made it. Tell your clients the truth and chances are good that they'll even help you in resolving the issue.

18

Don't blame someone else

I attended a meeting with one of my supervisors very early in my career. During the meeting, every time the client questioned what we had done, or pointed out some changes that needed to be made, my supervisor openly blamed one of my co-workers.

Now, I knew some of the things in question, my co-worker had done. Others, however, had been done at the direction of my supervisor. My supervisor blamed my co-worker for everything.

On the drive back to the office, I asked my supervisor about what had happened. He told me that the client didn't care who was responsible and would probably never meet with anyone else besides us. He said he needed to save face. He was surprised when I told him that I didn't think it was appropriate, that he was the client contact and responsible for directing the work. I also told my supervisor it was my belief that the client was probably turned off by him blaming someone else and not accepting responsibility for the firm's mistakes.

Have you ever interacted with someone and heard them blame some unnamed person back at the office for a situation?

Did you really care who was to blame?

By not taking responsibility for your actions, you send signals to your clients and your co-workers that you are not trustworthy. The client doesn't really care who caused the problem, he just wants to know that he can trust you to resolve the issue.

Blaming someone else undermines this trust.

19

It's not about who's right or wrong; it's about resolving the issue at hand

I'm sure you've heard the old adage "the customer is always right." While I don't subscribe to this holistically, there is some truth to the saying. Most of the time your client doesn't care who is right or wrong; he just wants the problem solved.

And here is the problem: too many professionals spend tremendous amounts of time trying to figure out who is right and who is wrong. Sometimes they spend more time than it's worth—they could've solved the original problem three times over instead of wasting valuable time.

How much time do you waste trying to prove who was right or wrong regarding an issue? The next time you run into an issue with something you are working on, try this:

solve the problem first, and then if it's still important to you, try to figure out what went wrong.

Unfortunately, in many organizations, people are punished for making a mistake. Your client may be a part of this type of organization. Solving the problem first allows him to keep the project moving and affords you the time to demonstrate you care about what you are doing. It also will go a long way toward building a solid relationship with the client.

After the issue is resolved, the client will be much more receptive to your needs and you'll be able to negotiate from a relationship-based position, not an adversarial one.

20

Be flexible. Each client's needs and projects are different

It's unfortunate that many professionals have such a rigid process model for the work they do. They make every client engagement go through the same hoops, even when those steps don't make sense for the client or for the project.

Be flexible in your approach to each client. Build upon the things you know, but look for opportunities to meet the client's specific needs. In more than twenty years in my profession, I have not found two clients who have the same goals or reasons for why they are doing a particular project.

I'm not saying that some things shouldn't be similar, but every time you try to solve today's problem with yesterday's knowledge, you will not reach your full potential. Moreover, your client will not feel that you are paying attention to his specific needs.

Look at each client and project as an opportunity to truly understand what that client is trying to accomplish—what is important to him—and figure out the best way to help him. Clients know when you are going the extra mile to uniquely address their issues, and they'll reward you for it.

Your flexibility in the engagement will result in a better project for your client and for you.

21

Don't lose touch after the job is done

During the course of doing a project with a client, you can develop close bonds. Clients appreciate this and come to like and respect you. Sometimes you even become close friends. How would you feel about a friend who only talks to you when he needs something? That's how a client can feel when you don't keep in touch after a job is complete.

Take the time to keep the relationship alive. It's good for you and it's good for business. I learned this lesson the hard way.

I had a client with whom I had developed a strong friendship. During the job, we enjoyed each other's company and talked about more than the current project; but for some reason, I didn't keep in touch with him after the job was complete.

I can't tell you how bad I felt when I drove by his office a couple of years later and saw a new expansion to his company's building being constructed, knowing didn't design it for them.

When I phoned the client, I found out that he perceived my friendship as only existing because we were doing work for him.

While I have been able to work through this issue with my friend, it still bothers me that I allowed our friendship to slip. It also hurt our business relationship—at least in the short term.

Stay in touch for the relationship.

Lastly...

I hope that this book, although very simple in its construction, helps you instill a stronger sense of the importance of providing exceptional customer service within your organization.

I have no doubt that you knew many of the points made here, but sometimes we get busy and forget.

Use this book as a reminder.

Use this book to teach others, for when you teach something, it then becomes knowledge. I challenge you to be the person who converts the information in this book to knowledge in your organization.

If you are not the right teacher in your organization, pass this book along to the one who is.

The sooner you start, the sooner you'll be on the path to creating more fulfilling and rewarding client relationships.

978-0-595-37365-9
0-595-37365-8

www.ingramcontent.com/pod-product-compliance
Lightning Source LLC
Chambersburg PA
CBHW021042180526
45163CB00005B/2242